Why can't I...
fly like a superhero?

and other questions
about movement

Sally Hewitt

Belitha Press

First published in the UK in 2001 by
Belitha Press Limited, London House,
Great Eastern Wharf, Parkgate Road,
London SW11 4NQ

ISBN 1 84138 185 3

British Library Cataloguing in Publication Data
for this book is available from the British Library.

Editor: Claire Edwards
Designer: Jacqueline Palmer
Picture researcher: Diana Morris
Consultant: Anne Goldsworthy

Printed in China

10 9 8 7 6 5 4 3 2 1

The bicycle on pages 16–17 was photographed
with the kind permission of Action Bikes,
176 High Road, Chiswick, London W4 1PR

Picture acknowledgements:

Brett Baunton/Stone: 12b background, 13c background.
R. Berenholtz/Stockmarket: f cover background, 10tr
background.
Ed Bock/Stockmarket: 21tr.
Manfred Danegger/NHPA: 8tr, 9tl, 28t, 30t.
Dimaggio/Kalish/Stockmarket: 14tr.
ExtraEye: 15tr.
Pictor International: 5 background, 9tr background,
23cr background.
Powerstock-Zefa: 23 background.
Eric Soder/NHPA: 8tl, 8ct.
Zefa-Mathis/Stockmarket: 11bl background.

All other photography by Ray Moller.

Every attempt has been made to clear copyrights.
Any omission is inadvertent and should be notified
to the publisher for correction in subsequent editions.

Contents

Why can't I fly like a bird?

Because you don't have wings.

Birds have very light bones
and strong muscles
for flapping their wings.

Your bones are much
heavier than a bird's.

You would need
very strong wings
to lift you
off the ground
and move you
through the air.

Why can't I fly like a superhero?

Because of gravity.

Gravity is a force.
You can't see it,
but if you try to fly,
gravity will always pull you
down towards the ground.

10

Why can't I float in the sky?

Because you are the wrong shape.

Without a parachute to slow you down,
gravity would pull you straight to the ground.

A parachute is a good shape
for collecting air. The air
stops you falling so fast
and lets you float down safely.

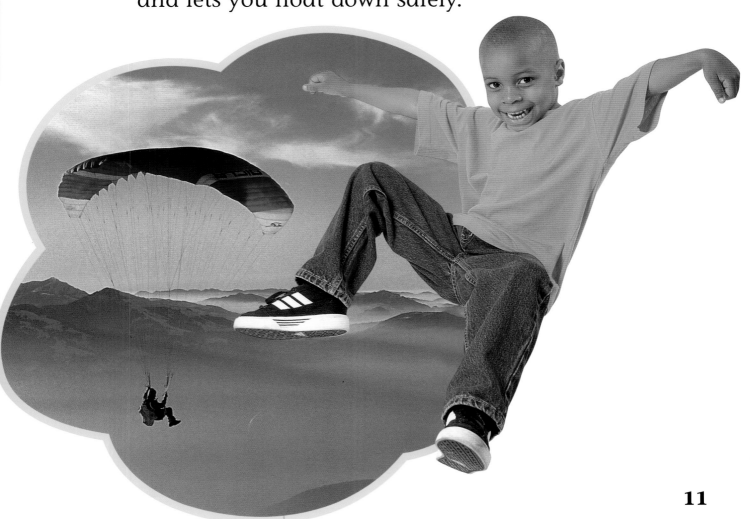

Why can't I toboggan uphill?

Because gravity will pull you and your toboggan downhill.

You have to push or pull
a toboggan uphill.
If you let it go, it slides back down
to the bottom of the hill again.

13

Why won't my truck move on its own?

Because nothing starts
to move all by itself.

You need to push
or pull your truck
to make it start to move.

If you put your truck
on a slope and let it go,
gravity will pull it down
the slope for you.

Why won't my boat sail without wind?

Because the wind blows into the sails and pushes the boat along.

Your boat won't start moving without a push from the wind.

Why do I have to pedal my bike?

Because a bicycle won't start to move by itself.

Pedalling is a way of pushing your bike along.

You have to pedal hard to go uphill, because gravity is pulling you downhill.

You can speed downhill
without pedalling at all!

Why can't I throw a balloon...

Because a balloon
is very light.

Even if you throw
a balloon very hard,
it will soon start to sink
to the ground.

as far as my ball?

Your ball is heavier
than a balloon.
When you throw it,
it will keep going
for longer.

19

Why can't I roller skate on square wheels?

Because square wheels won't roll along.

Circles are the best shape for turning round and round.

You can push heavy things more easily if you put them on wheels.

Why can't I slide on carpet?

Because your feet
and the carpet
rub against each other
and slow you down.

Ice skates slide over ice
because they are
both fairly smooth
and don't rub against
each other so much.

Why can't I squash a stone?

Because a stone is very hard.

You can squash clay because it is soft.
Once you have squashed clay,
it stays in its new shape.

22

Why do I leave footprints in the snow?

Because you sink into the snow.

You push down on the snow harder than the snow can push up on you.

23

Why can't I pick up food with a magnet?

Because food is not made of iron.

Magnets can pull metal things made of iron towards them.

They can pick up things such as pins and paperclips.

If a magnet could pick up your food, the food probably wouldn't be very good to eat!

Movement words

air You can't see air but it is all around you. Air pushes up on a parachute to slow it down as it falls.

force A force pushes or pulls on things to make them go faster or slower.

gravity Gravity is a force that pulls things towards the Earth and makes them fall down to the ground.

heavy Things that are heavy weigh a lot. Heavy is the opposite of light.

light Things that are light don't weigh very much. Light is the opposite of heavy.

magnet A magnet pulls things made of iron towards it. This force is called magnetism.

pull You can start something moving by pulling it towards you. A pull is the opposite of a push.

push You can start something moving by pushing it away from you. A push is the opposite of a pull.

squash You can squash or push a soft object made of something such as clay or sponge to change its shape.

stretch You can stretch or pull an object made of something such as clay or elastic to change its shape.

wind Wind is moving air. It can push things along.

How do you move?

Which of the words below would you use to describe the different ways you move in these everyday activities?

- Make a clay model
- Play football
- Clean your teeth
- Ride a bike
- Make your bed
- Write a letter
- Eat a meal

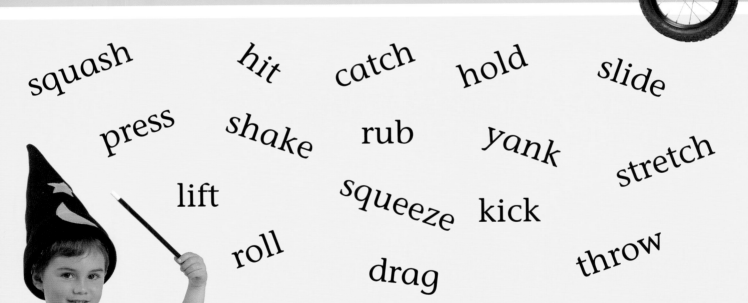

squash   hit   catch   hold   slide

press   shake   rub   yank   stretch

lift   squeeze   kick

roll   drag   throw

Can you work out which of these movements are pushes and which ones are pulls?

Think about all the things that move and what makes them move. Is there anything that never moves?

Notes for parents and teachers

Children know that they can't fly, but they may not know the reason why. Read the simple answers to the questions about movement, and then you may like to try out these activities with your child. They will help to reinforce the ideas in this book and give you plenty to talk about.

Heavy and light
Collect objects of different sizes and weights such as a balloon, an apple and some coins. Guess which are heavy and which are light. Pick them up and talk about how they feel. Put them in order of weight. Are big things always heavier than small things?

Fill some same-size food bags with different types of food, for instance potatoes, flour or pasta. Put two bags side by side and guess which one is heavier just by looking at them. Weigh them to find out if you were right.

Movement words
Make some jam tarts together and use movement words to describe what you are doing. Talk about when you are pushing and pulling. Shake the flour and watch it fall through a sieve. Rub the fat and flour to make crumbs; stir in a little water; push and squash the mixture into a ball; roll out the pastry; press the pastry cutter to cut the pastry.

Find some paper, some modelling material, a sponge, an elastic band, some cloth and a wooden brick. Notice and discuss what happens when you try to push, squash, stretch and fold them.

Falling down

Collect objects that can be dropped without breaking – such as a wooden brick, a sponge, a spoon, a paper tissue, a leaf and a piece of paper. One by one, hold them up high and drop them. Talk about how they fall. Do they fall straight down? Does the air seem to push up on some more than others? How can you tell? Do any go up? Why not?

Experiment with using a paper plate, a large handkerchief or some paper to make a parachute. Attach four pieces of string around the edges and tie on a small plastic toy. Which parachute works best?

Magnetism

Play with fridge magnets. Look for the little magnets at the back. Try placing the fridge magnets on different surfaces. Guess whether the magnet will be attracted to each surface.

Find a magnet and make a collection of small objects including several made of metal. Sort them into groups of the ones the magnet will pick up and those that it won't.

Index